P9-ECJ-300

GREAT BUDDHIST STORIES

Illustrations by Rob Koo

TREASURE
TOWER
BOOKS

Published by Treasure Tower Books
The children's book division of the SGI-USA
606 Wilshire Blvd.
Santa Monica, CA 90401

© 2011 SGI–USA

Illustrations by Rob Koo
Cover and interior design by Lightbourne, Inc.

All rights reserved
Printed in Korea

10 9 8 7 6 5 4 3 2

Library of Congress Cataloging-in-Publication Data

Great Buddhist stories / illustrations by Rob Koo.
     p. cm.
   Includes bibliographical references.
   ISBN 978-1-935523-22-2 (trade paper : alk. paper)
   1. Buddhist parables--Juvenile literature. I. Koo, Rob.
   BQ5780.G74 2011
   294.3'85--dc23

                              2011026062

INTRODUCTION

Buddhism is more than 2,500 years old. When it started, most people in India couldn't read, so the only way Shakyamuni Buddha could share Buddhism was to talk about it. Buddhists tell stories to teach the ideas of Buddhism. Sometimes we think of stories as being only for children, but these great Buddhist stories are for everyone.

Many of the stories in this book come from the early days of Buddhism. Nichiren Daishonin, who clearly explained the Buddha's main teaching as Nam-myoho-renge-kyo so everyone could practice it, also used stories a lot. In fact, most of the stories in this book are ones that Nichiren teaches, and in the back of the book you can read about where to find them. Buddhism may be old, but these stories can still teach us about what the Buddha understood. The stories talk about working hard, being grateful, generous and above all, understanding that all of us have a strong life inside of us—our Buddha nature—and we can bring it out by practicing Nichiren Buddhism in the SGI.

CONTENTS

The Poor Woman and the Lamp

A long time ago, Shakyamuni Buddha was coming to visit a city in India. The king of the city, who was very rich, bought oil and a thousand lamps as presents for the Buddha.

An old woman who lived in the city wanted to buy something for the Buddha as well, but she was very poor and lived all alone. Still, she thought: The Buddha is a great person who wants to help all people. I'd really like to offer him a gift.

She had nothing to sell but her hair, so she cut off her hair and sold it to a wig maker. This gave her enough money for one oil lamp. She gave this lamp to the Buddha.

That night, a storm came. Winds rushed through the city and blew out every one of the king's thousand lamps. Of all the lamps, only the lamp given by the sincere old woman stayed lit, all night long.

GREAT BUDDHIST STORIES

In the Lotus Sutra, Shakyamuni tells his disciples the story of **"THE JEWEL IN THE ROBE."**

One night, two friends had dinner together. One of them was very rich; the other was poor.

They drank some wine ...

and the poor man went to sleep.

The rich man had to leave to take care of his business far away,

and out of concern for his friend,

he sewed a precious jewel into his friend's robe.

The poor man, after he woke up, went to look for food. He found a little food here...

... a little food there.

He thought it was OK to live that way.

When the rich man returned, he asked his friend, "Did you not see the jewel I gave you?"

The poor man had no idea of the wealth he'd had all along.

Shakyamuni told this story to show that we all carry the precious gem of Buddhahood inside, though often unaware of it.

GREAT BUDDHIST STORIES

THE DRAGON GATE

Nichiren Daishonin told his disciples about an amazing waterfall in China, called the Dragon Gate.
It's extremely high, and the water rushes down faster than an arrow. At the bottom of the falls, carp live in a pool. It is said that if a carp swims up the waterfall, it will become a dragon! Dragons are strong and quick, and they have the power to control the weather. But the carp are small, and the waterfall is quite high for them. Not only that, as the fish struggle and swim up, eagles swoop down and try to eat them. Fishermen throw nets and spears at the carp, too. Some of the carp try for years and years to make it up the waterfall.

GREAT BUDDHIST STORIES

Bodhisattva Never Disparaging

In the Lotus Sutra, there is a story about a bodhisattva named Never Disparaging. He never made fun of people or put them down. He always sought the Buddha nature in all people and in all life. Everywhere he went, he'd bow and say to people ...

I would never be disrespectful to you, because you are a Buddha.

Some thought: Who does this guy think he is? Nobody can be that nice!

Why, I never!

Yet, even when people were mean to him ...

Curse you!

The Six Wise Men and the Elephant

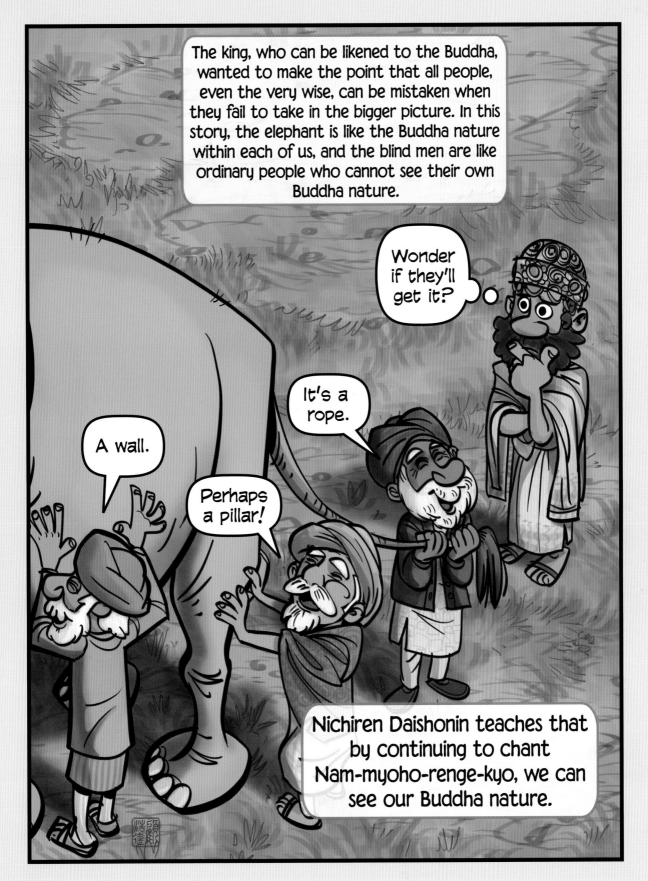

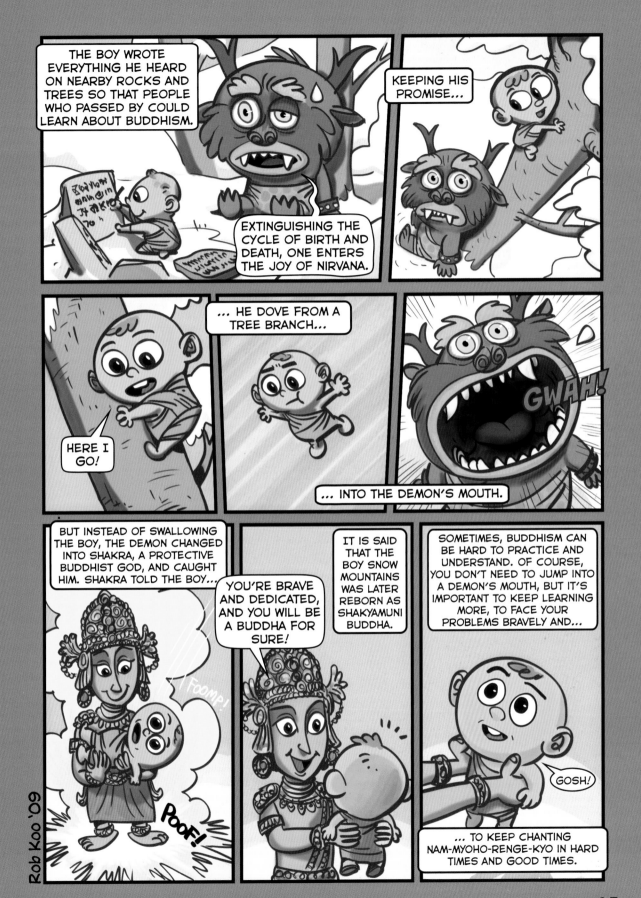

GREAT BUDDHIST STORIES

THE DRAGON GIRL

THE DRAGON KING LIVED AT THE BOTTOM OF THE SEA. HIS EIGHT-YEAR-OLD DAUGHTER STUDIED THE LOTUS SUTRA AND WAS ABLE TO SHOW SHAKYAMUNI'S DISCIPLES HOW THE LOTUS SUTRA CAN BRING OUT THE BUDDHAHOOD IN ALL PEOPLE.

A DISCIPLE NAMED MANJUSHRI SAID...

SHE'S REALLY COOL. SHE COULD BECOME A BUDDHA RIGHT AWAY.

NO WAY...

SAID BODHISATTVA WISDOM ACCUMULATED...

IT TAKES A MILLION-FRILLION-BAJILLION LIFETIMES TO BECOME A BUDDHA.

A GIRL CAN'T BE A BUDDHA. A DRAGON IS AN ANIMAL AND CAN'T BE A BUDDHA.

A DRAGON GIRL DOUBLE CAN'T BE A BUDDHA, SO THERE!

SURE I CAN BE!

GREAT BUDDHIST STORIES

VIRTUE VICTORIOUS AND THE MUD PIE

A BOY NAMED VIRTUE VICTORIOUS WAS PLAYING OUTSIDE WHEN SHAKYAMUNI BUDDHA CAME TO TOWN.

TO HELP PEOPLE BECOME HAPPY, SHAKYAMUNI TRAVELED A LOT. AND SINCE HE DIDN'T HAVE MUCH, PEOPLE OFTEN GAVE HIM FOOD.

THE BUDDHA LOOKED SO KIND AND WISE, AND VIRTUE VICTORIOUS WANTED TO OFFER HIM A GIFT.

BUT HE HAD NOTHING TO GIVE.

SO, VIRTUE VICTORIOUS SCOOPED UP SOME MUD...

... AND MADE A PIE OUT OF IT.

SHAKYAMUNI SMILED, APPRECIATING THE BOY'S DEEP SINCERITY.

BECAUSE OF THE SINCERE GIFT OF THIS MUD PIE, IT IS SAID THAT VIRTUE VICTORIOUS BECAME A GREAT BUDDHIST KING IN HIS NEXT LIFETIME. HE WAS CALLED KING ASHOKA, ONE OF THE GREATEST KINGS IN THE HISTORY OF INDIA. ALL PEOPLE HAVE THE BUDDHA NATURE INSIDE. ONE IMPORTANT WAY WE EXPRESS IT IS BY SINCERELY SHOWING RESPECT TO PEOPLE, JUST AS VIRTUE VICTORIOUS DID.

Rob Koo '10

GREAT BUDDHIST STORIES

THE COLD-SUFFERING BIRDS

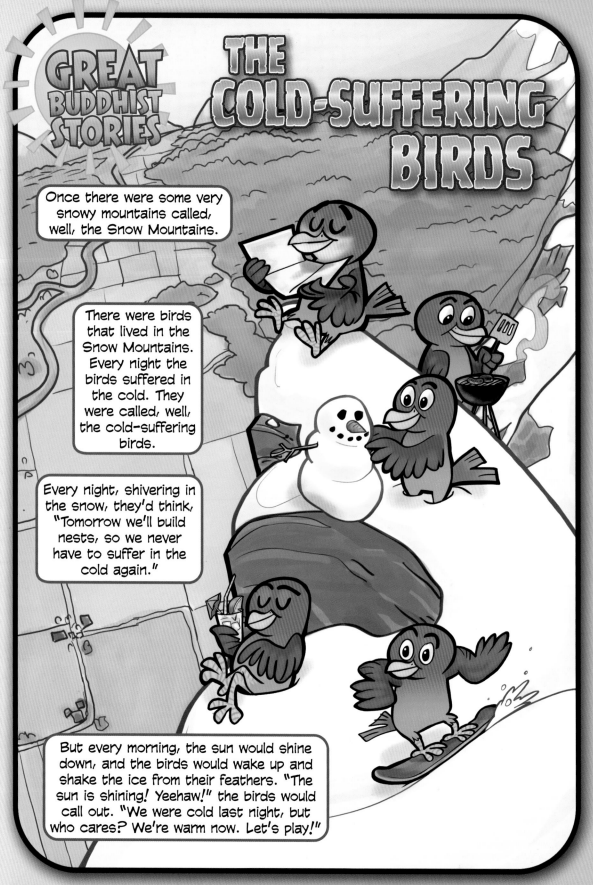

Once there were some very snowy mountains called, well, the Snow Mountains.

There were birds that lived in the Snow Mountains. Every night the birds suffered in the cold. They were called, well, the cold-suffering birds.

Every night, shivering in the snow, they'd think, "Tomorrow we'll build nests, so we never have to suffer in the cold again."

But every morning, the sun would shine down, and the birds would wake up and shake the ice from their feathers. "The sun is shining! Yeehaw!" the birds would call out. "We were cold last night, but who cares? We're warm now. Let's play!"

General Stone Tiger

A long time ago in China, a young man named Li Kuang lived with his parents in a small village.

One night, a tiger sneaked into the village and ate Li Kuang's mother.

Li Kuang decided right away to hunt down the dangerous tiger. Night and day he searched for the tiger, determined to get him.

母親 MOTHER

TWANG!

Then, under the moonlight, Li Kuang saw the tiger in the distance. He drew his bow, aimed with total concentration and shot the arrow.

To his surprise, he found that he hadn't hit a tiger at all, but instead had hit a big rock. Li Kuang's determination had been so strong that he'd shot the arrow right into the rock.

The arrow went in all the way to the feathers!

Li Kuang came to be known as General Stone Tiger.

TWANG!

SNAP!

But you know what? When he tried later on to shoot the rock again, knowing that it was a rock and not a tiger, the arrows bounced off.

Buddhism teaches that to do amazing things, we have to be really determined. Like Li Kuang when he shot the arrow into the rock, we should chant Nam-myoho-renge-kyo and take action with fierce determination that we will achieve our goal.

MAO PAO & THE WHITE TURTLE

A well-dressed young man named Mao Pao went for a walk by a riverbank. There, he saw a fisherman catch a white turtle in his net. Mao Pao felt sorry for the turtle.

Please, Mister Fisherman, let the poor turtle go!

No way, rich boy, I need money, and I can sell him.

To win the turtle's freedom, Mao Pao gave his own nice clothing to the fisherman, so the fisherman could sell them instead of the turtle. The fisherman let the turtle go, and the turtle swam away.

Many years later, Mao Pao became a brave soldier. One day, while in battle, his enemies chased him.

He ran and ran.

They chased Mao Pao to a riverbank.

Even though the water was rough and cold and dangerous, he jumped in to get away from his enemies. Mao Pao was sure he would drown.

But then, he felt something carrying him across the river to safety. The white turtle had remembered him!

Nichiren Daishonin says we should always remember to be grateful to those who help us. Just as the turtle never forgot Mao Pao's kindness, we should never forget those who are kind to us.

THE FOUR MEETINGS

GREAT BUDDHIST STORIES

Siddhartha was a wealthy young prince who lived in a fine palace in northern India. He was handsome, educated and had little to worry about.

EASTERN GATE

Why do people grow old?

One day, taking a walk through the palace's eastern gate, he saw a very old man.

SOUTHERN GATE

COUGH! COUGH!

Why do people get sick?

Another day, he left from the southern gate and saw a sick person.

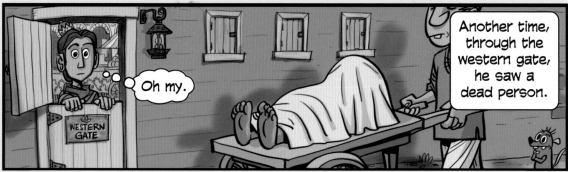

WESTERN GATE

Oh my.

Another time, through the western gate, he saw a dead person.

Everyone who is born will age, get sick and die eventually... Everyone!

This worried and puzzled the young prince.

On yet another walk, he met a wise man near the northern gate. The wise man's attitude and behavior impressed the prince.

These things made Siddhartha think deeply about life. Soon, he left the palace and all his riches. He even gave up the possibility of being king. Instead, he chose to go on a journey to study, so that he could one day become wise enough to understand the four sufferings—birth, aging, sickness and death.

And you know what? He did come to understand them! He eventually became known as Shakyamuni Buddha. A Buddha is a person who understands these things perfectly. Shakyamuni then taught people how to overcome these sufferings. But, that is another story.

Illustration by Rob Koo

Chudapanthaka

In the days of Shakyamuni Buddha, there lived two brothers named Mahapanthaka and Chudapanthaka— Maha and Chuda for short.

Maha decided to become a Buddhist and found Buddhist teachers to tell him about it.

Chuda came with him.

Maha was smart and learned about Buddhism quickly.

But Chuda had a very hard time learning. He just couldn't remember or understand the things he was taught. Sometimes he couldn't even remember his name.

He actually forgot his own name!?

REFERENCES

The Poor Woman and the Lamp
"Reply to Onichi-nyo," *The Writings of Nichiren Daishonin*, vol. 1, p. 1089

The Jewel in the Robe
The Lotus Sutra and Its Opening and Closing Sutras, p. 190

The Dragon Gate
"The Dragon Gate," WND-1, 1002

Bodhisattva Never Disparaging
LSOC, 307–13

The Phantom City
LSOC, 154–81

The Six Wise Men and the Elephant
"Letter from Teradomari," WND-1, 208

The Boy Snow Mountains
"The Fourteen Slanders," WND-1, 755–61

The Dragon Girl
LSOC, 226–28

Virtue Victorious and the Mud Pie
"The Two Kinds of Faith," WND-1, 899

The Cold-suffering Birds
"Letter to Niike," WND-1, 1027

General Stone Tiger
"General Stone Tiger," WND-1, 952–53

Mao Pao & the White Turtle
"The Opening of the Eyes," WND-1, 244

The Four Meetings
See *The Living Buddha* by Daisaku Ikeda, pp. 16–17

Chudapanthaka
"Lessening One's Karmic Retribution," WND-1, 199